THE BUSHCRAFT HANDBOOKS

FOOD & WATER
IN THE BUSH

Illustrations by the Author

Richard H. Graves

The Bushcraft Handbooks
Food & Water in the Bush

This Edition Copyright © 2013 by Palmer River Publishing

Cover, Graphics and Layout by: Palmer River Publishing

ISBN-13: 978-1484813591
ISBN-10: 1484813596

About The Author

The author of "The Bushcraft Handbooks", Richard Graves, is a member of the Irish literary family of that name.

A veteran of the Great War campaigns in the Dardenelles and the Western Front, the author became passionate about the bush at an early age. As an enthusiastic bushwalker, skier and pioneer of white-water canoeing, he foresaw how a knowledge of bushcraft could save lives in the Second World War. To achieve this end, he initiated and led the Australian Jungle Rescue Detachment, assigned to the Far East American Air Force. This detachment of 60 specially selected A.I.F. soldiers successfully effected more than 300 rescue missions, most of which were in enemy-held territory in New Guinea, without failure of a mission or loss of a man.

An essential preliminary for rescue was survival, and it was for this purpose that the notes for these books were written. These notes were later revised and prepared for a School in Bushcraft which has been operating for several years and continues to provide valuable instruction to Servicemen embarking overseas on active service in Korea and Malaya.

Bushcraft

As far as is known, "The Bushcraft Handbooks" are unique. There is nothing quite like them, nor is any collection of published bushcraft knowledge as comprehensive.

The term "Bushcraft" is used because "woodcraft" commonly means either knowledge of local fauna and flora or else is associated with the blood-sports of hunting and shooting. "The Bushcraft Handbooks" include a volume on traps and snares, but these are purposely-designed to be completely ineffective for native animals which are insect enters or grazers. These traps have been included because they would only be effective in catching predatory animals such as cats and dogs which have taken to the bush, and other "pest" creatures such as feral swine or goat.

"Bushcraft" describes the activity of how to make use of natural materials found locally in any area. It includes many of the skills used by primitive man, and to these are added "white man" skills necessary for survival, such as time and direction, and the provision of modern "white man" comforts as illustrated in the volume on bush campcraft.

The practice of bushcraft develops in an individual a remarkable ability to adapt quickly to a changing environment. Because this is so, the activity is a valuable counter to the over-specialisation so prevalent in today's society, and is particularly significant in youth training and character-moulding work.

INTRODUCTION to the BUSHCRAFT HANDBOOKS

THE PRACTICE OF BUSHCRAFT shows many unexpected results. The five senses are sharpened, and consequently the joy of being alive is greater.

The individual's ability to adapt and improvise is developed to a remarkable degree. This in turn leads to increased self-confidence.

Self-confidence, and the ability to adapt to a changing environment and to overcome difficulties, is followed by a rapid improvement in the individual's daily work. This in turn leads to advancement and promotion.

Bushcraft, by developing adaptability, provides a broadening influence, a necessary counter to offset the narrowing influence of modern specialisation.

For this work of bushcraft all that is needed is a sharp cutting implement: knife, axe or machete. The last is the most useful. For the work, dead materials are most suitable. The practice of bushcraft conserves, and does not destroy, wild life.

R.H.G.
April, 1952

THE BUSHCRAFT HANDBOOKS

CONTENTS

FOOD & WATER IN THE BUSH

Many people associate survival with the ability to find food and water. These of course are essential to sustain life.

In all areas, except the most arid, food and water in sufficient quantities are available, but the fear in many people's minds is that the food they find may be poisonous, or the water polluted.

This handbook establishes safe principles for recognising foods which are edible and safe, and ways to overcome possible contamination of water, no matter how badly it may appear polluted.

The search for, and recognition of edible foods sharpens and develops three of man's senses, sight, taste and smell. On the use of these depends the searcher's success in finding food and water.

Associated with the finding of natural foodstuffs which are edible and safe, is the preparation of these.

Bearing in mind that the person concerned with survival may have no equipment except a knife or machete, the cooking of food and boiling of water may be no less important than the actual finding of these. It is for this reason that these subjects are included in this book.

Food and water are essential to living. Under normal conditions a person cannot live longer than three days without water, but one can live ten days or longer without food.

1

Food, apart from its vitamins, mineral salts and other minute elements, must contain Proteins and Carbohydrates. Proteins are the flesh builders. Carbohydrates are the energy makers—the fuels for your body's furnace.

Every action calls for work from some of your body's cells, and, although new cells are continually being made in your body tissue, old cells are dying. These body tissue cells require replacing, and it is the digestible protein in your food which is used to build these cells.

PROTEINS are supplied by such foods as meat, cheese, nuts, beans and peas.

CARBOHYDRATES are supplied from the starchy foods such as bread, sugar, potatoes, and roots and tubers, and green vegetables and sweets generally, including honey.

For every action you burn up fuel. The more vigorous your actions the more fuel you require, and the faster your body burns it. This fuel is supplied from the carbohydrates in your food. Your body can no more run without this fuel than can the engine of a car if the petrol tank is empty. Your body stores up in its cells reserves of sugars, so that even if you have no food for your stomach, you can draw on these reserves and keep going for a short period.

Your body also needs other foods such as salt and special minerals and vitamins, but in a natural diet most of these essential specialities are contained in the fruits and meats and vegetables which you would eat.

It is possible to have a full stomach at every meal and at the same time to starve to the point of death. If you tried to live entirely on proteins, you might starve for carbohydrates, and, correspondingly, you could be full of carbohydrates but starved for proteins. There should be a balanced proportion of proteins to carbohydrates, and the proportion is, roughly, one part of protein to six parts of carbohydrates.

Another absolute daily essential is salt. Without sufficient salt there can be serious physical consequences. In tropical areas where there is great loss of body salt through excessive perspiration, it is essential to eat salt, and maintain the salt content of the blood at a safe level.

IMPORTANT

General rules covering the edible qualities of foods are set out in the succeeding sections. If there is doubt, take no risk. Eat a small quantity of the suspected food, and await results. If there are no ill-effects the food is probably safe.

All Flesh is Edible

Nearly all flesh, if freshly killed, is safe to eat. The flesh of all mammals, all reptiles and all birds is free from any poisonous contents and safe. But NOT the flesh of all fish.

By "poisonous" is meant actually toxic, that is, containing a poison. An exception in the reptile world is the Hawksbill turtle, which, in the thorax, contains a sac which more learned authorities class as toxic or poisonous.

Parasite Infestations

The words "safe to eat" do not mean that the flesh may be eaten with no ill-consequences. It merely means that the flesh itself contains nothing which will be poisonous to adult human beings.

Many animals are hosts to parasites which can be fatal to man if they are introduced into his body. For instance, the flesh of the rabbit may be infested with hydatids, a worm which, if it finds entry into a human, can often prove fatal. The ancient Jewish law which declared the pig unclean was undoubtedly based on the observation that eaters of pig meat showed a higher death rate than eaters of other meats. Pigs are commonly infested with parasites which can also make man their host. Hence the law forbidding the eating of pig flesh.

In common with the pig and the rabbit there is always the chance that the flesh of almost any animal (particularly animals which graze close to the earth, or which burrow or which frequent fresh water streams) may be infested with parasites dangerous to man, and consequently no flesh is absolutely safe to eat raw, even in emergency. However, the parasites and their eggs are destroyed by heat, and therefore all flesh should be thoroughly cooked before eating.

This particularly applies to all fresh water fish and fresh water shellfish.

Bacterial Decay

Putrefaction and decay are caused by bacterial action. Food is protected commercially by freezing, by salting or pickling, by heating and canning, and by many other means. None of these methods which call for equipment are practical in the bush, therefore other methods must be found to preserve meat safely for indefinite periods.

Meat goes bad because of bacterial infection. Bad meat can be fatally poisonous if eaten. When the term "safe to eat" is used it only applies to freshly-killed and fresh meat.

Preserving Meat for Long Periods

The preservation of meat for long periods can be done by smoking and sun-drying, by salting and pickling and, for short periods, by cooking in fat. If climate permits, meat can also be preserved indefinitely by freezing.

Sun-Drying (Biltong)

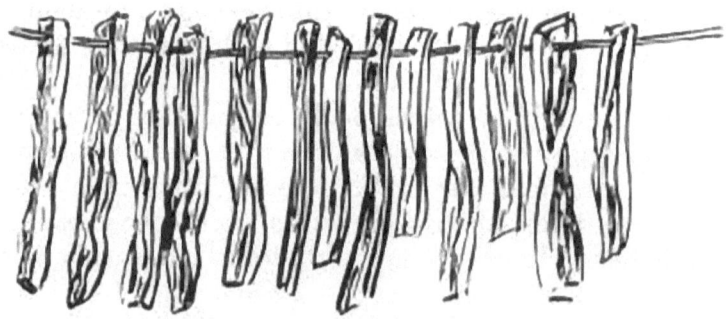

The meat to be smoked or sun-dried must be freshly killed. Cut off the fatty portions, and then slice the meat into strips no thicker than half an inch and no wider than one inch. These strips are threaded on to a wire or cane, so that no piece of meat touches another.

There must be free circulation of air round each separate piece.

Hang the canes or wires with the strips of meat above the thin blue smoke of a wood fire until the outer surface is quite dry. This may take from an hour to a day. Do not allow the meat to hang too close to the fire, or in the flame. Smoke alone is sufficient. If the meat is to be sun-dried, the only reason for hanging in the smoke is to protect the moist meat from blowflies while the outer surface is drying.

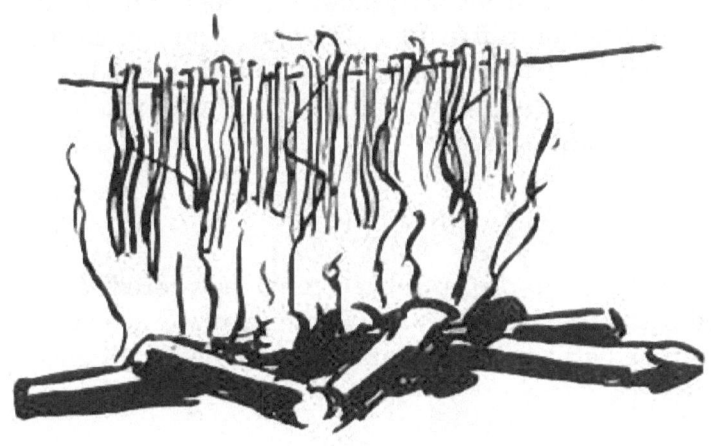

It is also important not to try and build a "smoky" fire by piling on green leaves or wet rubbish. If you do the moisture and essential oils evaporated from the leaves will condense on the strips of meat and make it uneatable.

Many an enthusiastic but inexperienced meat drier has ruined his meat by making a fire of green leaves, and then wondered why the meat was saturated with oil from the leaves.

Blowflies will not lay their eggs, or their larvae, on a dry surface. When the surface is quite dry, take it from the fire and hang it in the sun to complete the drying process.

A single day in a dry atmosphere will complete the drying-out. When carrying dried meat, pack it in a bag of open weave. Do not wrap or pack in cellophane or plastic, otherwise the meat will "sweat" and mildew.

Sun-dried or smoked meat will keep indefinitely and retain its original nutritive food value. You can cook it in a stew, use it for broth, or eat it raw. If well smoked, it is very palatable eaten raw. When using for a stew, it is advisable to soak for an hour or two.

Pemmican

This is simply sun-dried meat powdered. It may be mixed with fat in cool climates. Pemmican will keep very well, and can be eaten raw, or soaked and made into hamburgers or stews.

Drying and Weight

These simple methods of preserving flesh effect a considerable reduction in weight, simply because the excess moisture has been removed.

This is important to the traveller who goes through the bush on foot. About six ounces of dried fish or meat is equivalent to one pound of fresh meat. There is also a corresponding reduction in volume.

Dried Fish (Edible Fish)

The fillets of fish which it is known are safe to eat may be sun-dried in a similar manner to meat. With fish it is essential to dry quickly, and, if the day is not hot and dry, then smoke thoroughly over the fire. If the flesh is flaky and cannot be cut into strips, heat flat smooth stones and lay the slices of flesh on these, and place in the sun to dry out thoroughly. Turn the slices frequently. Fish meat is easily powdered into fish pemmican, and can be cooked either by making into fish cakes, or by soaking, if in strips, and then frying in batter.

By keeping the fish strips in the smoke continuously until they are completely dry, you have smoked fish, and very nice too! The best smoke for this is a thin blue smoke, and definitely not a heavy white smoke.

Pickling

The meat is cut into small joints or pieces of about half a pound each, and put in a strong solution of salt and water (brine). Pickled meat will keep indefinitely in the brine.

Cooking in Fat

Meat can be preserved up to five or six days in summer by preliminary cooking in fat, and then allowing the meat to remain in the fat in which it was cooked. The heat of cooking sterilises the meat, and the fat seals the meat safely away from bacterial infection. This method is convenient when meat requires to be kept for a short period.

Fat

When sun-drying meat, it is necessary to remove the fatty portions before drying, otherwise the fat will go rancid and taint the dried meat, making it uneatable. The fat should not be thrown away. Fat is food, and the fat cut off the meat should be rendered down and kept, if possible, as dripping for future use.

Freezing

Freezing as a means of preserving meat is not practical unless in a climate where the temperature can be relied upon to remain below 29 to 30 degrees. Freezing alone is an excellent way to keep meat and is often used during winter ski-ing trips.

Preliminary Cooking

Meat which has been either boiled or baked has in the boiling or baking been made sterile, that is, the bacteria which cause putrefaction have been destroyed, and therefore the meat will remain safe to eat for a short time. Re-cooking will effect further sterilisation and prolong the period during which the meat can be eaten. The time between cooking and the meat being unsafe to eat depends largely upon the weather; hot humid conditions will make the meat unsafe more rapidly than cool dry conditions.

The presence of blowfly grubs or maggots on meat does not mean that the meat is tainted and unsafe. These maggots do not indicate poisonous properties of decay in the meat. Their presence merely indicates the visit of the female fly, which, seeing suitable conditions for her eggs or larvae, has placed them there where they may have food. Meat which has been blown can be washed and eaten with perfect safety. Admittedly the maggots are repulsive, but they are in themselves quite free from actual poison. The blowfly is no guide to the condition of meat. It will blow any meat, putrefied and poisonous or safe.

Edible - But Not Palatable

To say that meat is safe to eat does not mean that it is palatable. The flesh from a shag or diver (cormorant) is edible, but so strongly "fishy" and "oily" that it is most unpalatable. Nevertheless, in emergency it can provide the proteins necessary to sustain life, and this flesh is wholly digestible.

The flesh of a cat, dog or rat is edible, and if you did not know the origin of the meat prior to its being cooked, you would eat it without repugnance. Cat tastes almost exactly like hare. Flying fox, roasted, is as succulent as sucking pig; and snake, roasted in the ashes, has a white meat of delicate flavour. But you would not say they were palatable, simply because the source of the meat to your mind would be repulsive.

The rule is that the flesh of all birds, mammals and reptiles is safe to eat, but not all are palatable.

All Water Creatures

The flesh of some sea creatures is dangerous to eat because the flesh contains actual toxins poisonous to your digestive system.

Saltwater Fish

Provided the fish have the usual appearance of fish, and have scales and the conventional shape of a fish, you can say that it is safe to eat and has no poisons in the flesh.

If the creature does not have the usual "fish shape," and does not have scales, then regard it as poisonous, unless you know for certain that it is safe. An example is the shark, which has no scales. The flesh of the shark is safe to eat, but beware of the "innards." Shark liver has such a high concentration of vitamin D that a feed of shark liver, fried, might be fatal. The eel, which does not have the conventional shape of a fish, nevertheless has minute scales (or so I read somewhere), and the flesh is safe to eat. Properly cooked, it is most palatable, though somewhat rich in flavour.

The puffer or toady, the box fish, the pig fish and the leatherjacket do not have the conventional fish shape, nor do they all have the scales of a fish, and are all poisonous, except the leatherjacket, and I should be doubtful about eating the roe (eggs) or liver.

Colour of the flesh is no indication of the presence of poison in the flesh. Many of the parrot fish, having the fish shape and scales, have green flesh, yet all are edible and very palatable. It is interesting to note that many ancient mariners, including Captains Cook and Bligh, report that their men "caught a mess of brilliant fish from the sea, and after cooking same were violently ill, being taken with great pains, and they fell a-vomiting, being purged with the poison of the fish they had eaten."

It has since been noted by many observers that putrefaction of the flesh of many tropical fish sets in a few minutes after the fish has died. Consequently, the poisonous property attributed to the flesh is in reality due to the fish having gone bad in a few minutes. (The author has identified many of these tropical fish once thought to be poisonous; cooked immediately they have been caught, they have been eaten with no ill-effects. At the same time, some of the same catch were kept uncooked; in half an hour they were bad.)

You should reject for food any fish which lacks scales or which is of unusual shape, unless you know for certain it is safe to eat. ('Safe' includes eels, sharks, and rays, the flesh of all of which is edible, but do not under any consideration eat the 'innards'.)

Shellfish

All bivalves are free from toxic poisons, except for a reputed poison in the saltwater mussel at certain periods of the year, and the flesh of all is safe to eat, unless taken from contaminated waters.

Pippie

Clam

Cockle

This particularly applies to freshwater shellfish, which are likely to be hosts for parasite infestations which can be harmful to man.

Those taken from freshwater should be well cooked to destroy any possible parasites and their eggs, also the source of the fresh water stream should be known to be reasonably free from sewage contamination.

When the flesh is tough, it can often be made tender enough for eating by beating.

Cooking can be either by boiling, grilling or baking.

Bivalves

Bivalves are found all along the coastal sea beaches. They make an excellent meal. A dozen to eighteen bivalves are a good feed for one person. To cook, put the bivalves in a billy and pour boiling water on them. The bivalves will open, and the fish itself can be easily removed from the two shells. The fish must be washed several times in water to remove all sand, and then boiled in fresh water, add milk and thickening after boiling (or water and dried milk if desired) for ten minutes. Before cooking, the flesh may be cut into small pieces. After ten minutes' boiling, add thickening and salt to taste. Pippie soup is identical with the famous New Zealand Toheroa soup, only it doesn't cost so much and you get more toheroa!

Oysters

Oysters, of course, are eaten raw, or they may be cooked and served as soup. Oysters are edible and safe all the year round.

Clams

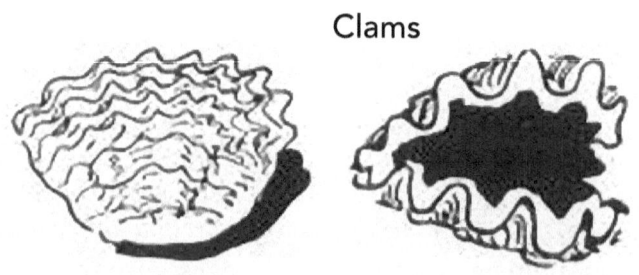

Clams and most of the other bivalves must be cooked. The big clams of the Barrier Reef are all edible and there are records of captains of ships, long forgotten, sending men ashore to the Reef to collect clams, and detailed accounts of the cooking of them. Practically all these accounts state the clams were boiled before eating.

Conical and Spiral Shellfish

Abelone

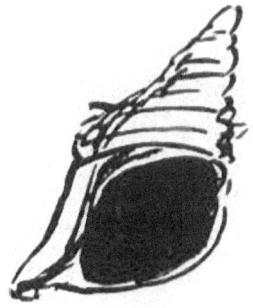

Whelk

Conus

The flesh of all the conical and spiral shellfish is edible and free from toxic poisons, with one exception, and many are very palatable.

The exception is one family of spiral cone-topped shellfish, the "Conus" family. Many of these have a poison dart or tongue which can inflict a very painful wound (one known fatality was at Hayman Island in 1935). These poisonous "conus" family of shellfish are not usually found out of tropical waters. They can be identified by the spirally-shaped conical top of the shell.

Abelone

Particularly recommended for food are Abelone (Haliotis). These are a flat spiral up to five or six inches in length and four to five inches across, by about an inch and a half high.

These are invariably found below low tide level and like a position on rock among kelp and long seaweeds. They have some mobility and move sluggishly around the rock. They can be found by feeling gently among the weeds. They feel like a roundish part of the rock and, if taken suddenly, can be pulled free. However, if given a chance to clasp the rock with their myriads of suction cup "feet" they cannot be pulled free with the hand, and a knife must be inserted under the shellfish to lever it loose.

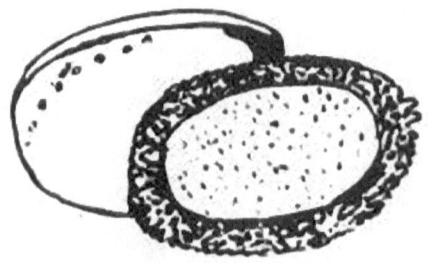

Shell

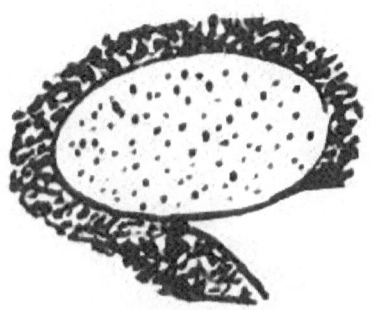

Meat (remove shaded portion)

To cook abelone, remove the shellfish from the shell, cutting the muscle at the top of the shell. Remove the intestines, and with a sharp knife trim off the ridge with the suckers, scrape off the blackish lining, and the base of the fish where it is rough from the rock face.

Beat the remaining portion heavily, and then toast on both sides till brown. Eat with salt to taste. Two are an adequate meal for one person.

The flavour is rather sweet, like lobster meat, only very much richer.

Another method of cooking is to cut into small half-inch squares after beating and allow to stand for about half an hour. The abelone "bleeds" with a bluish juice. Boil in this juice for five minutes, add milk and thickening and salt to taste, and boil for a further five minutes. May be eaten hot on bread or toast, or served cold as a savoury. The flavour either way is excellent.

Native people cooked abelone by dashing the fish down sharply on its back immediately it is taken from the water and then tossing the shell and fish on to a fire of hot coals and baking in the shell.

Whelks

These large shellfish measure up to five or six inches in length and are found in rock pools among kelp and seaweed. The flesh itself is too tough to eat even when beaten. Break the shells open with a rock and remove the shellfish entire. Put these in water and boil for ten minutes and then strain off the liquid into another billy and add milk, thickening and salt to taste. The result is a really delicious soup. The flavour is identical with crab, very rich, and most palatable.

Crustaceans

All the crustaceans are safe to eat and free from toxic poisons, but freshwater crayfish and yabbies are subject to parasite infestations which may be harmful to man, and therefore the flesh should be extremely well cooked as a safety measure.

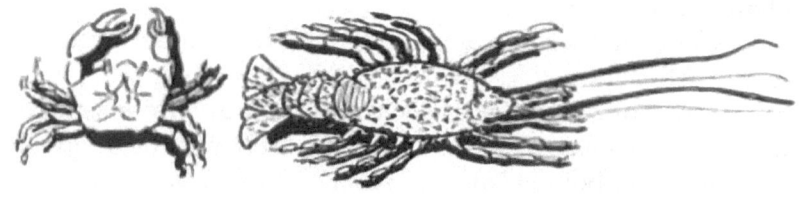

Crustaceans are usually boiled, but it is quite practical to simply kill the creature and wrap the shellfish in either an old wet newspaper, a ball of clay or large green leaves, such as banana leaves or palm leaves. The wrapped shellfish is then placed deep in the hot ashes of a fire. Be sure you place it in the ashes, and not the surface coals. Cover the bundle completely and leave for six to twelve hours. The food will not have burnt or dried out, but will be cooked deliciously.

This is an excellent means of cooking all meats. Freshly-killed wild duck, pigeons and all fresh meat is tough. If cooked in the ashes for ten to twelve hours the meat, how-ever, will be tender. The meat cannot burn because the temperature of the ashes is slowly reducing all the time. This is an excellent way to cook large fish in camp.

Octopods and Gastropods

The flesh on the tentacles of all the octopods and gastropods (octopus and cuttlefish, etc.) is edible, but many are extremely tough and rubbery. The flesh of octopus tastes exactly like lobster. To cook, beat the octopus tentacles and boil in very hot oil, 10-15 minutes. It is probable that there are other ways of preparing these for food, because they are a favourite delicacy among Mediterranean peoples.

Caution: one small species of ringed octopus–4" to 6" long–has been known to give fatal stings.

Insects

Some of the insects are a valuable source of food. Consider the bee and the food value of its honey.

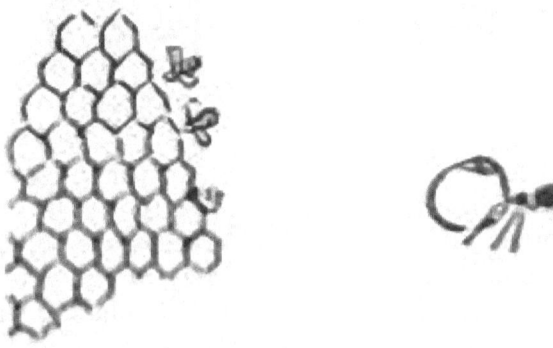

Honey is so rapidly assimilated by the body that, if given by any means to a person unconscious from exhaustion, it will be almost immediately assimilated and restore consciousness and strength.

Honey is probably the most valuable single natural food for an emergency ration, and certainly the best "energy-giver" for walkers and climbers, except for glucose and

17

proprietary products of a kindred nature.

In addition to the bees, certain species of ants store honey in their bodies, and have marked food value, and the wood grub (the "witchetty grub" of the blacks) is a delicacy when toasted, if one can overcome a natural prejudice. This is simply a matter of mental conditioning.

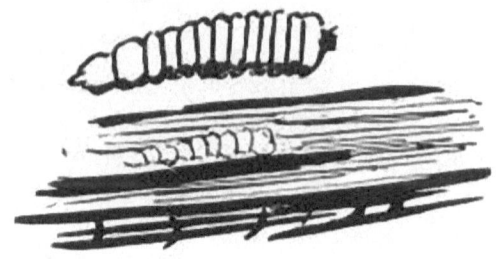

Vegetable Foods

Grasses, Ferns and Herbage

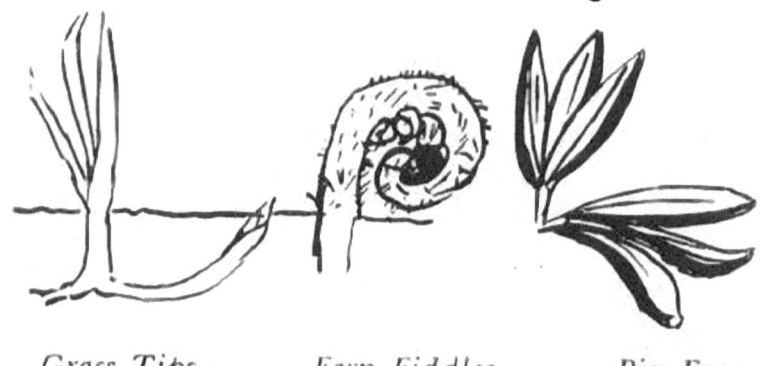

Grass Tips   *Fern Fiddles*   *Pig Face*

The young whitish tips of all grasses are edible, and most are very palatable and tender. They can be eaten raw, and have a' considerable food value. This applies to bamboo, which is botanically a giant grass. The seeds of all grasses are edible, and a valuable protein source. '

The young fiddles of many of the ferns are regarded as edible, but only a few are palatable, and many have a tendency to "scour." Bracken tips are edible, but are not recommended for food by this writer.

Leaves of many forms of herbage are edible and very palatable. The plants specially recommended are Tetragonia. sometimes called New Zealand spinach, and sometimes miscalled "saltbush." This plant grows all along the sub-tropical coastal areas. It may be recognised by its light-green, slightly fleshy leaves (petiole in shape, that is, similar to an ivy leaf), and small yellow flowers. Tetragonia may be eaten raw or boiled. It is very palatable and has fair food value.

Pig Face

Pig Weed

PIG FACE (Mesembryanthemum)

These are all edible raw and most have a high moisture content and a tendency to act as a mild purgative. Food value is low, but they could sustain life. Baked, they are good food.

PIG WEED
This is edible and good food.

WATERCRESS

This grows in most of the fresh water courses, along the edge of streams. It makes an excellent salad eaten raw, has a slightly "hot" taste, and when freshly picked is crisp and nourishing. A word of warning. This plant may harbour one of the freshwater snails, which is host to some of the flukes or parasitic worms. Do not take a chance; wash the leaves thoroughly before eating.

STINGING NETTLES

These are edible and very palatable, but, of course, they cannot be eaten raw. Boil for ten minutes before serving. Nettles are grown in gardens in France for food. They must be picked with gloves on, and if gloves are not available, pull a sock over one hand and so protect your skin from the poison spines.

Do not confuse these ground nettles with the Nettle Trees or Stinging Trees of tropical areas.

Fruits, Leaves and Roots

There are two fairly common poisons in the vegetable world. Fortunately, both are easily identified by taste.

One has the taste of a bitter almond or a peach leaf.

This is hydrocyanic or prussic acid, a potent and highly dangerous poison which is often water soluble. When you find this taste in a plant, whether leaf, root, seed or fruit, suspect the plant as a source of food in the raw state, unless you know it is safe to eat.

If this poison is present, try boiling some of the plant, and then taste after boiling. If the "almond" taste is no longer noticeable, then you may regard the plant as probably safe to eat after boiling.

It is unwise to eat a large meal of the plant after this test. It is far safer to eat a small portion, and then wait a half hour. If there are no signs of stomach ache, vomiting or sickness, then you can be quite certain that the food is now safe.

The symptoms are stomach pains, nausea, and vomiting. Poisoning can be serious. Antidotes would be alkalis such as milk or soda (the white ash from a fire is soda ash and would serve as an antidote if mixed with water).

The other poison is recognised by a sharp stinging, burning or hot sensation caused by tiny barbs irritating the tongue, throat, lips and palate. This poison, for example, is found in the stalk of the arum lily. It is an oxylate of lime crystal. It can be exceedingly painful, causing swelling of the tongue, throat and lips. In general, oxylate of lime crystals are not water soluble.

If this poison is detected in a test tasting of a plant, reject the plant out of hand. The poison cannot be removed, and the plant is not edible.

Bitterness or Extreme Acidity

Avoid any plant which is bitter or very acid or very 'hot'. The unpleasant taste is a certain danger signal.

RED is a Danger Sign

The colour RED associated with a plant in tropical or sub-tropical areas can be regarded as a danger signal. Any plant which shows red in any part of its growth, in its fruits, in its leaves, or in its stalks should be regarded with suspicion unless you know for certain that it is absolutely safe.

For example, the strawberry (an alpine fruit originally) is known to be safe to the general run of people, but some unfortunate folk are very sick if they eat strawberries.

RHUBARB LEAF

Rhubarb has a red stalk, but the leaves are deadly when cooked because they contain a fatal quantity of oxalic acid.

The tomato belongs to the solanum family, the same family of plants as the deadly nightshade. So, in a general way, be suspicious of any plant which shows the danger signal red, unless you are absolutely certain that it is safe to eat. This is particularly applicable to tropical berries and fruits.

Another general sign of probable poison is any fruit which is divided into five divisions. This is a generalisation, but it is better to be cautious than overbold—and poisoned.

Leaves

The leaves of many trees, shrubs and ground plants are edible, and very palatable, and can comfortably sustain life.

The only test is to taste the leaf. If it is tender and pleasant to the palate and the danger tastes of almond, bitter, or extreme acid are not present, then you can eat a small quantity, and if there are no ill-consequences, then the leaves of that particular tree or shrub are safe and will be good food for you.

The leaves of most plants contain oil cells which give the leaf its taste or flavour. This is generally more marked in the young leaves at the end of branchlets.

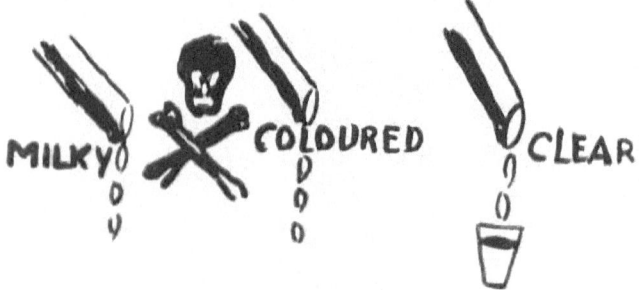

Beware of all trees which have a coloured sap, white, red or black. Many of these saps are a danger signal, and some, particularly the white saps, can inflict painful burns to the skin or, if allowed in the eye, can cause blindness. Also beware of the ground trefoils, particularly those which have little corms or tubers. These are generally Oxalis, and have a dangerously high content of oxalic acid.

Fungi

All forms of fungus growth should be avoided. The food value is negligible, and unless you know for certain that a particular fungus is safe to eat, do not touch it. The fungus plants contain poisons which affect the nerves by causing paralysis. Many are extremely dangerous and to date very little is known of them. The author has had some small experimenting in this field and found a few, apart from the common "mushroom," which are very palatable and quite safe. One of the best of these is the puffball in its very early stage of growth before the ball itself has dried and become puffy.

The writer's advice is: "Leave all the fungus growth severely alone."

Arctic Berries

In the cold climates most berries are edible. This is in contrast with tropical and sub-tropical areas, where berries generally should be regarded as probably poisonous. In tropical areas the colour red is always a danger signal, and a good rule is to avoid all red berries. This does not apply in the colder climates, where almost all red berries are edible. Poisons are liable to be present in berries and this general rule should be observed in regard to all unknown berries.

Seeds and Nuts

A few seeds contain deadly poisons, and these poisons may not always be detected by the palate. In general, a bitter, strongly acid, or burning "hot" taste is a sign of poisonous contents. Any seeds with these tastes should be avoided. The mere act of tasting will not affect you. The poison may be tasted but must not be swallowed. When you are testing seeds to see if they are edible, you can spit out the portion you have tasted if it is unpalatable, and there will be no ill-effects.

Nuts, of course, are seeds, but for this work have been separated into a different section. Many nuts contain hydrocyanic acid poison. This is always detected by the palate, and in nearly all instances where it occurs it can be dissolved by either boiling or soaking in water for 10 to 12 hours. Other nuts, such as the candle nut–a relative of the tung nut–are violent purgatives. Again, cooking either by boiling or baking may render them harmless. Unless you know for certain that the nuts are safe to eat, regard them with some suspicion and test by first tasting, and if taste indicates no poison, then eat a small quantity. If there are no ill-effects within an hour, the nut will be safe.

Roots and Tubers

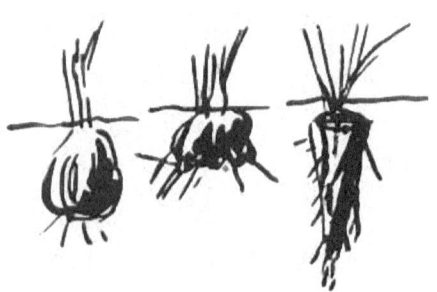

Most of the roots and tubers are safe, but almost all must be either boiled or heat treated in some way before they are digestible. The common potato is almost valueless as a food unless cooked.

Yams are not a particular species of plant. The word "yam" simply means the root of a ground vine. The sweet potato is a yam. They are a prolific source of food among people in tropical and sub-tropical regions. There are many vines which have these ground tubers, and, as far as is known, all such tubers are edible if free from the oxylate of lime crystals. In most yams the hydrocyanic poison is water soluble. Although the botanical genus of these tuber-yielding plants will vary greatly, there is one factor in common in the veining system of the leaf. This must not be taken as a hard and fast rule, but it is a very good guiding principle. If the leaf shows that the veins radiate from the point of juncture of the leaf with the stalk, rather than from a main vein, then there may be tubers to be dug from the species of plant.

The tubers and bulbs of many plants are edible, and the simple test of tasting for hydrocyanic acid or oxylates of lime crystal can be applied to all with a fair degree of reliability.

Remember that your own body normally provides you with the safeguards. First is the sight of your food. If it looks healthy and clean, it may be all right. The sense of smell is your next safeguard. If the food smells all right, you apply the next safeguard and taste it. If the taste is all right, the food probably is safe.

The principle of edible foods is as simple as that.

Remember to be careful with nuts and seeds; to regard red as a danger signal; and to avoid the fungi. If you remember these three rules you will undoubtedly be quite safe in testing and eating most plants which are palatable.

Water

Associated directly with food is water. These two are essential to life. Just as there is the problem of finding food in the bush, so too is there the problem of finding water, and many explorers and backwoodsmen died because they did not know how or where to look for water in apparently dry and arid regions.

Many different forms of life are certain indicators of water in the near vicinity. The bees must have water. The mason fly, that big yellow and black hornet-like creature, requires mud and water for the tunnel wherein he stores the spider he has paralysed. Pigeons and all grain eaters need water, but the flesh-eaters such as the crow and the hawks and eagles can go without water for long periods. By knowing something of the nature of the insects, birds, animals and reptiles you can often find their hidden stores of precious water.

Insect Indicators of Water

BEES
Bees in an area are a certain sign of water. Rarely will you find a hive of wild bees more than three or four miles from fresh water. A bee flies a mile in 12 minutes. You can be sure that if you see bees you are not far from fresh water, but you will probably have to look for further indications before you actually find the water supply.

ANTS
Many of the ants require water, and if you see a steady column of small black ants climbing a tree trunk and disappearing into a hole in a crotch it is highly probable that there will be a hidden reservoir of fresh water stored away there. This can be proved by dipping a long straw or thin thick down the hole into which the ants are going. Obviously if it is wet when you draw it out there is water there. To get the water do not on any account chop into the tree. If the hole is only very small, enlarge it with your knife-point at the top. Make a mop by tying grass or rag to a stick. Dip the mop into the water and squeeze into a pannikin. Another method is to take a long hollow straw and suck the water you require from the reservoir. These natural tree reservoirs are very common in dry areas, and are often kept full by the dew which, condensing on the upper branches of the tree, trickles down into the crotch and so into the reservoir inside the tree. Water reservoirs are very common in the she-oaks (casuarinas) and many species of wattle.

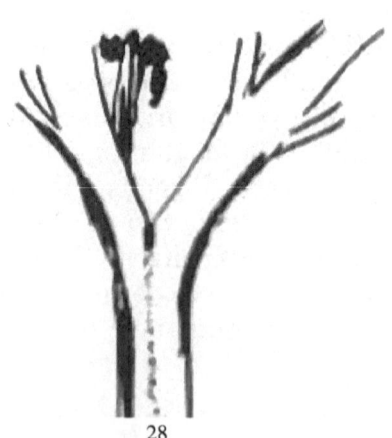

MASON FLIES

These large, hornet-like creatures are a certain indicator of water. If you see a mason fly's buildings in an area you can be sure that you are within a few hundred yards of a soak of wet earth. Search around carefully and you will see the mason fly hover and then suddenly drop to the ground. If you examine the place where she landed you will find the soil is moist, and that she is busy rolling a tiny pellet of mud for her building. By digging down a few inches (or at most, a couple of feet) you will assuredly find a spring and clear, fresh, drinkable water.

Bird Indicators of Water

FINCHES

All the finches are grain-eaters and water-drinkers. In the dry belts you may see a colony of finches and you can be certain that you are near water, probably a hidden spring or permanent soak.

WILD PIGEONS

Wild pigeons are a reliable indicator of water. Being grain and seed eaters they spend the day out on the plains feeding, and then, with the approach of dusk, make for a waterhole, drink their fill, and fly slowly back to their nesting places.

Their manner of flight tells the experienced bushman the direction of their water supply. If they are flying low and swift they are flying to water, but if their flight is from tree to tree and slow, they are returning from drinking. Being heavy with water, they are vulnerable to birds of prey. It is obvious then that the direction of water can be discovered by observing the pigeons' manner of flight.

GRAIN EATERS

All the grain eaters and most of the ground feeders require water, so that if you see their tracks on the ground you can be reasonably certain that there is water within a few miles of your location. An exception to this are parrots and cockatoos, which are not regarded as reliable indicators of water.

FLESH-EATING BIRDS

The carnivores, being flesh eaters, get most of the moisture they require from the flesh of their prey, and consequently are not reliable water-drinkers. Therefore, do not regard the presence of flesh-eating birds as an indicator of water in the area, nor should you regard the water living birds as indicators of fresh or drinkable water.

Mammal Indicators of Water

Nearly all mammals require water at regular intervals to keep themselves alive. Even the flesh eaters must drink, but animals can travel long distances between drinks, and therefore, unless there is a regular trail you cannot be confident of finding water where you see animals' trails. This is a general rule. However, certain animals never travel far from water. For example, a fresh track of a wild pig is one sign that there is water in the vicinity, also the fresh track of 'roos-and most of the grazing animals, whose habit it is to drink regularly at dawn or dusk. In general, water will be found by following these trails downhill.

Reptile Indicators of Water

Most of the land-living reptiles are independent, to a very large extent, from water. They get what they require from dew and the flesh of their prey, and as a result are not an indicator of water in the area.

Water from Vegetable Sources

The roots and branches of many trees contain sufficient free-flowing fluid to relieve thirst, and this can be collected by breaking into 3 ft. lengths the roots or branches and standing these in a trough (of bark) into which the collected fluid will drain to the pannikin. In some plants the amount of water stored is truly unbelievable, the fluid literally gushing out when the plant is cut.

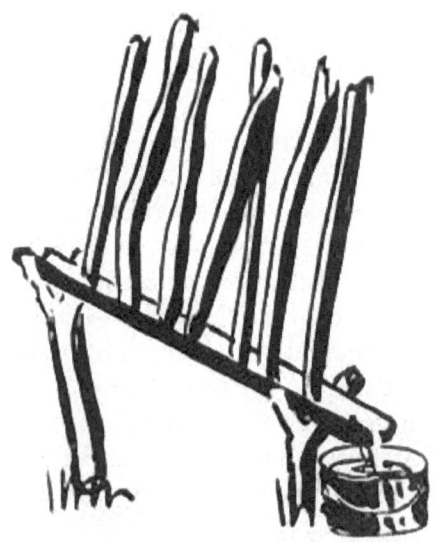

These vegetable "drinking waters" cannot be kept for more than twenty-four hours. The fluid starts to ferment or go bad if stored, and might be dangerous to drink if in this condition.

The nature of the plant, if judged by the properties of its foliage, is no guide to the drinkability of the fluids which are its sap. For example, the eucalypts, whose leaves are heavily impregnated with oils of eucalyptus, and in many cases poisonous to human beings, contain a drinkable fluid, easily collected (from the branches or roots). This fluid is entirely free from the essential oils and with no taint of the eucalyptus.

The lianas or monkey ropes found in tropical areas are an example of a prolific source of water.

There are certain precautions, and a few danger signs, with regard to vegetable fluids. If the fluid is milky or coloured in any way, it should be regarded as dangerous, not only to drink but also to the skin. Many of the milky saps, except those of the ficus family, which contain latex, or a natural rubber, are extremely poisonous. The milky sap of many weeds can poison the skin and form bad sores, and if allowed to get into the eye may cause blindness and severe pain.

With all vegetable sources of fluid even though the water itself is clear, taste it first and, if quite, or almost, flavourless, it is safe to drink.

For vegetable sources of water in arid areas the best volume is generally obtained by scratching up the surface roots. They are discovered close to the ground, and if cut close to the tree, may be lifted and pulled, each root yielding a length of from ten to twenty feet. These must be cut into shorter lengths for draining.

Many people who have tried to obtain drinking water from vegetable sources failed to get the precious liquid to flow because they did not break or cut the stalk or root into lengths. Unless these breaks are made, the fluid cannot flow, and the conclusion is that the root, branch or vine is without moisture.

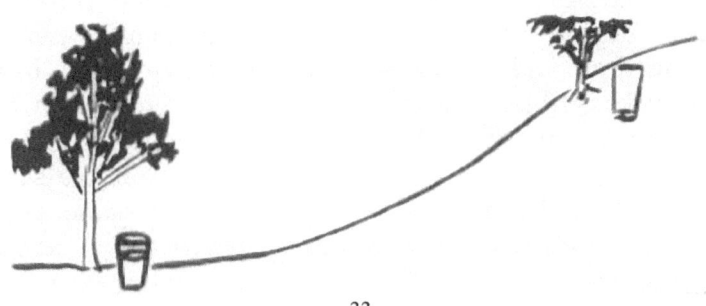

In general, water is more plentiful from plants in gullies than on ridges, and the flow is wasted if the roots are broken into sections and not cut. Cutting tends to bruise and seal the capillary channels.

Dew Collection

In barren areas where there are no trees, it may be possible to collect sufficient moisture from the grass in the form of dew, to preserve life. One of the easiest ways of dew collection is to tie rags or tufts of fine grass round the ankles and walk through the herbage before the sun has risen, saueezing the moisture collected by the tufts or rags into a container. Many early explorers saved their lives by this simple expedient.

Pig Face (Mesembryanthemum) and Ice Plant (Parakylia) and Pig Weed contain large proportions of drinkable moisture.

Water on the Sea Coast

Fresh water can always be found along the sea coast by digging behind the wind-blown sandhills which back most ocean beaches. These sandhills trap rain water, and it floats on top of the heavier salt water which filters in from the ocean. Sandhill wells must be only deep enough to uncover the top inch or two of water. If dug deeper, salt water will be encountered and the water from the well may be brackish and undrinkable. It will be noticed, too, that the water in these wells rises and falls slightly with the tides.

These sand wells are a completely reliable source of water all over the world. When digging it is necessary to revet the sides with brushwood, otherwise the sand will fall into the well.

On coastal areas where cliffs fall into a sea a careful search along the lower edges of the cliff will generally disclose soaks or small springs. These in general follow a fault in the rock formation and frequently are evident by a lush growth of ferns and mosses.

Moisture from Fish Flesh

Another source of liquid sufficient to sustain life at sea, when fresh water has ceased to be available, is from the flesh of fish. The fish are diced, and the small portions of flesh placed in a piece of cotton cloth and the moisture wrung out. This moisture from sea fish is not in itself excessively salty, and can sustain life for a long period.

Condensing Salt Water

It is possible to condense sea water without equipment and obtain sufficient fresh water for drinking purposes. (See moisture condensation overleaf.)

A coolamin is made, or alternatively a hole is scraped in the ground and lined, and the salt water is put into this hole. A fire is built, and stones are put in the fire to heat. These when hot are put in the salt water, which soon boils, and the water vapour is soaked up by a towel or thick mat of cloth. In time, this will literally become saturated, and may be wrung out, yielding a fair quantity of fresh drinkable water. Once the cloth is damp and cool, the collection of water vapour is fairly rapid.

Moisture Condensation in Arid Areas

A simple still for water condensation in arid areas can be made from a piece of light, waterproof sheeting, about 4 ft. square.

A hole is dug or scooped in the ground in a sunny position. The hole should be about 3 ft. across and 15" to 18" deep or deeper if possible.

The site should preferably be in moist ground, a depression in a creek bed is ideal if one can be found. If green material such as shrubs or succulent herbage is in the vicinity, the hole should be lined with this and the material packed down. It may be necessary to weigh the material down with a few flat stones.

In the centre of the hole, and in the deepest part, a billy or container is placed to catch the moisture collected by condensation.

Lay the sheet of plastic to cover the top of the hole, and weigh the edges with stones and use some of the earth scooped from the hole to seal the edges lightly. Place a stone in the centre of the upper side of the plastic sheet above the approximate centre of the water container to weigh it down to just over the container.

Moisture in the soil, and in the greenery placed in the hole will be drawn off by the heat of the sun and condense on the underside of the plastic. Condensation results because the air above the plastic is considerably cooler than the air on the underside of the plastic. The condensed moisture will collect into droplets, coalesce and trickle down the underside to the lowest point where it drops off into the container.

If the underside of the plastic sheet is slightly roughened with fine sandpaper or a similar fine abrasive such as a piece of finely grained stone, the droplets will coalesce and run off more cleanly than if the underside is absolutely smooth. Body waste, such as urine, waste food, moist tea leaves, etc., can be put in the hole. The pure moisture only is condensed. From one to four or five pints of water a day can be collected by this method. If the stay in the area is likely to be of some duration the top few inches of the hole can be removed and fresh green material replaced and the still will continue to work when this is done. Fresh still sites may be necessary every second or third day.

Acknowledgement: This effective method was first evolved by the Water Conservation Laboratory in Arizona.

Stagnant Water

Stagnant water, or water which has become polluted, can be made drinkable and pure without equipment.

If time permits, such water can be filtered through a sieve of charcoal.

This will both clarify and to a large extent purify the water, but it is always safer to boil it before drinking.

If the water is muddy, the clay particles in flotation in the water can be precipitated by a pinch of alum, which will flocculate and precipitate the particles and so clarify the water. This, however, requires at least 12 hours' wait.

If no artificial means are available, the polluted or dirty water can be filtered by straining through closely woven garments such as a felt hat or a pair of thick drill trousers. The water, if polluted, can be sterilised by adding hot stones to the water in the filter. The water will soon boil and so made sterile and safe for drinking.

In areas where there is a likelihood of water being infected with bacteria, it is always advisable to boil before drinking or, failing this, to chlorinate the water with a pinch of chloride of lime.